Easy to Play Viola Airs and Ballads

Gene
Clarke

MEL BAY

WWW.MELBAY.COM

Foreword

Many beautiful melodies—both folk songs and "composed" popular songs—originated in Great Britain and the United States during the nineteenth and early twentieth centuries. *Easy to Play Viola Airs and Ballads* is a collection of twenty-five of these tunes arranged in a way that can be enjoyed by student and amateur violists of all ages.

All the tunes are written entirely in first position, with bowing indications and fingerings for any unusual accidentals marked. Chord names are included for accompaniment by a guitarist or player of any chord-capable instrument. Every song can also be played along with the corresponding title in *Easy to Play Violin Airs and Ballads* and *Easy to Play Cello Airs and Ballads.*

I thank Mr. William Bay for encouraging me to write this book and helping me find the tunes herein. I hope all of you enjoy playing these melodies as much as I have enjoyed collecting, arranging, and playing through them!

Gene Clarke

Contents

Fingerpicking or Strumming

All the Pretty Horses

Traditional Lullaby
arranged by Gene Clarke

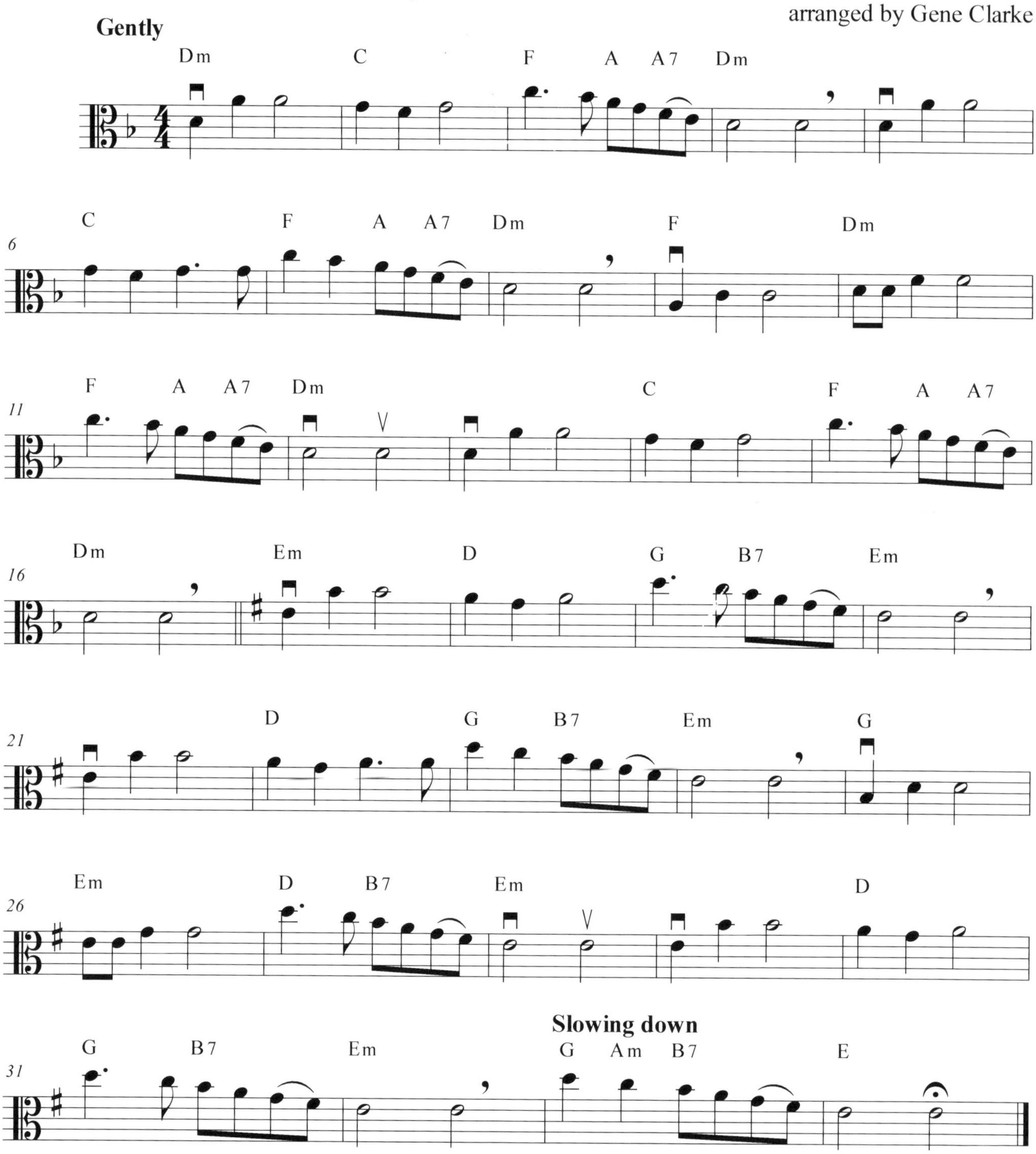

Barbara Allen

Traditional Scottish Balled

arranged by Gene Clarke

Slowly and sadly

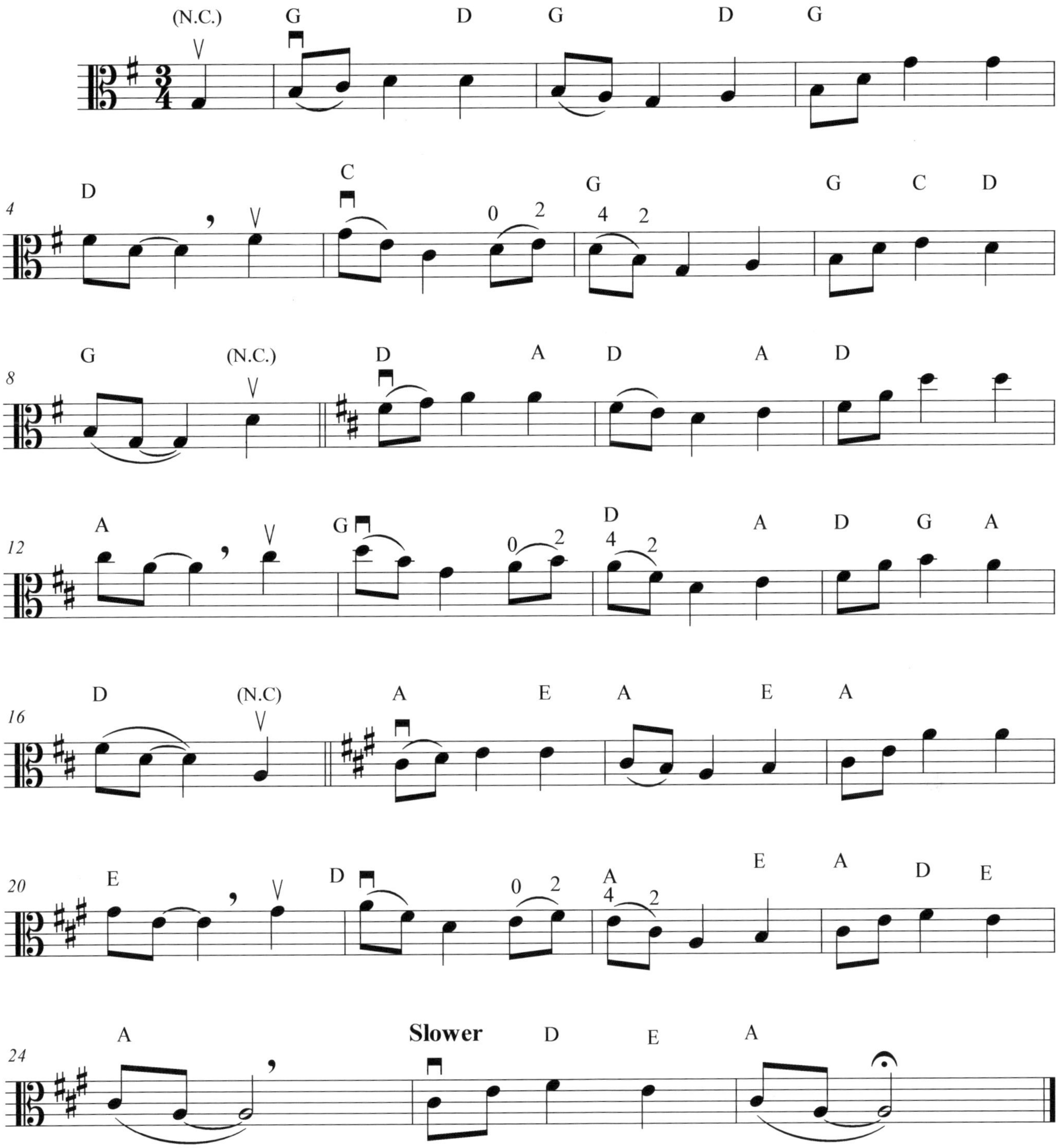

Bonnie Dundee

Scottish Folk Tune
arranged by Gene Clarke

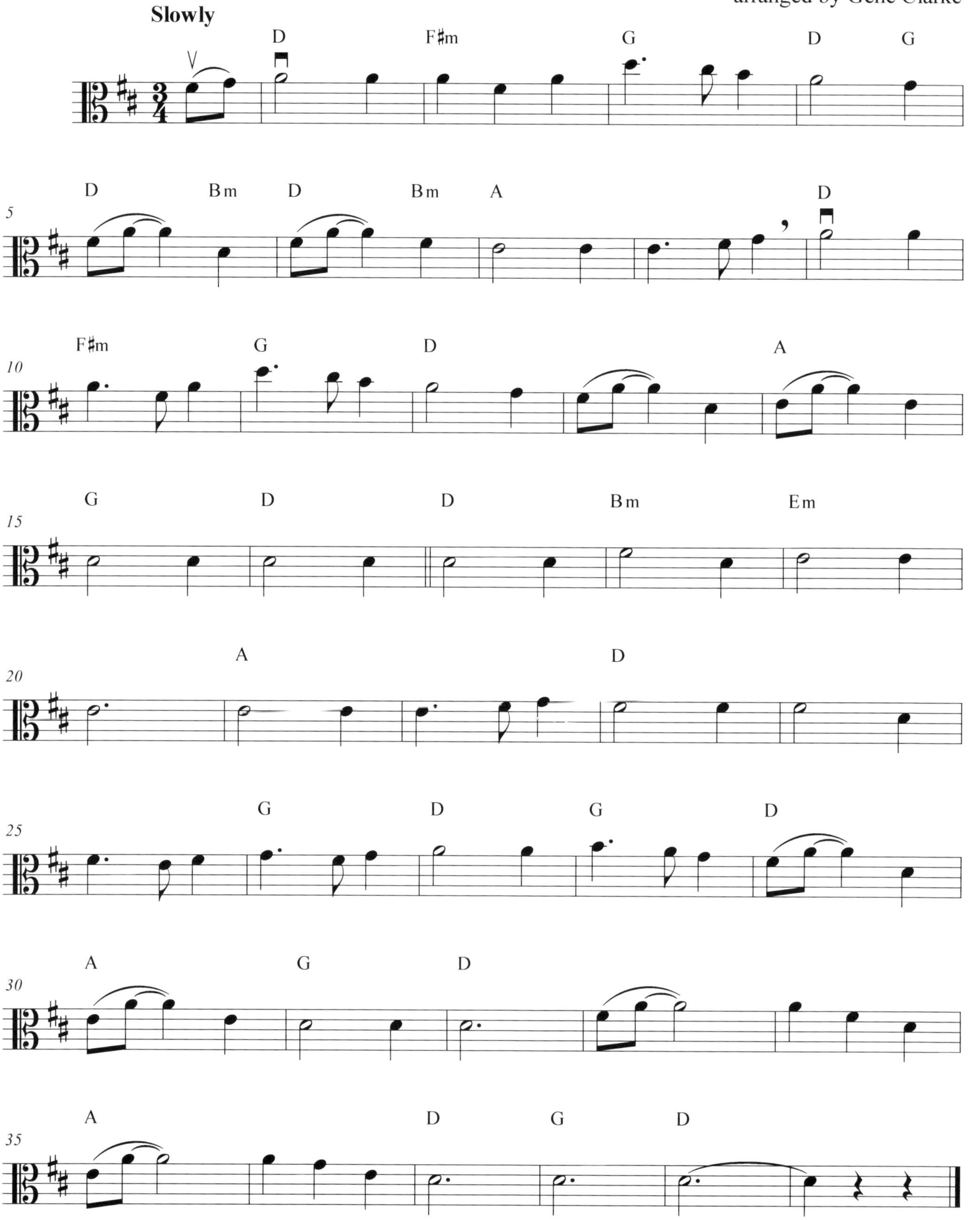

Botany Bay

Australian Folk Song
arranged by Gene Clarke

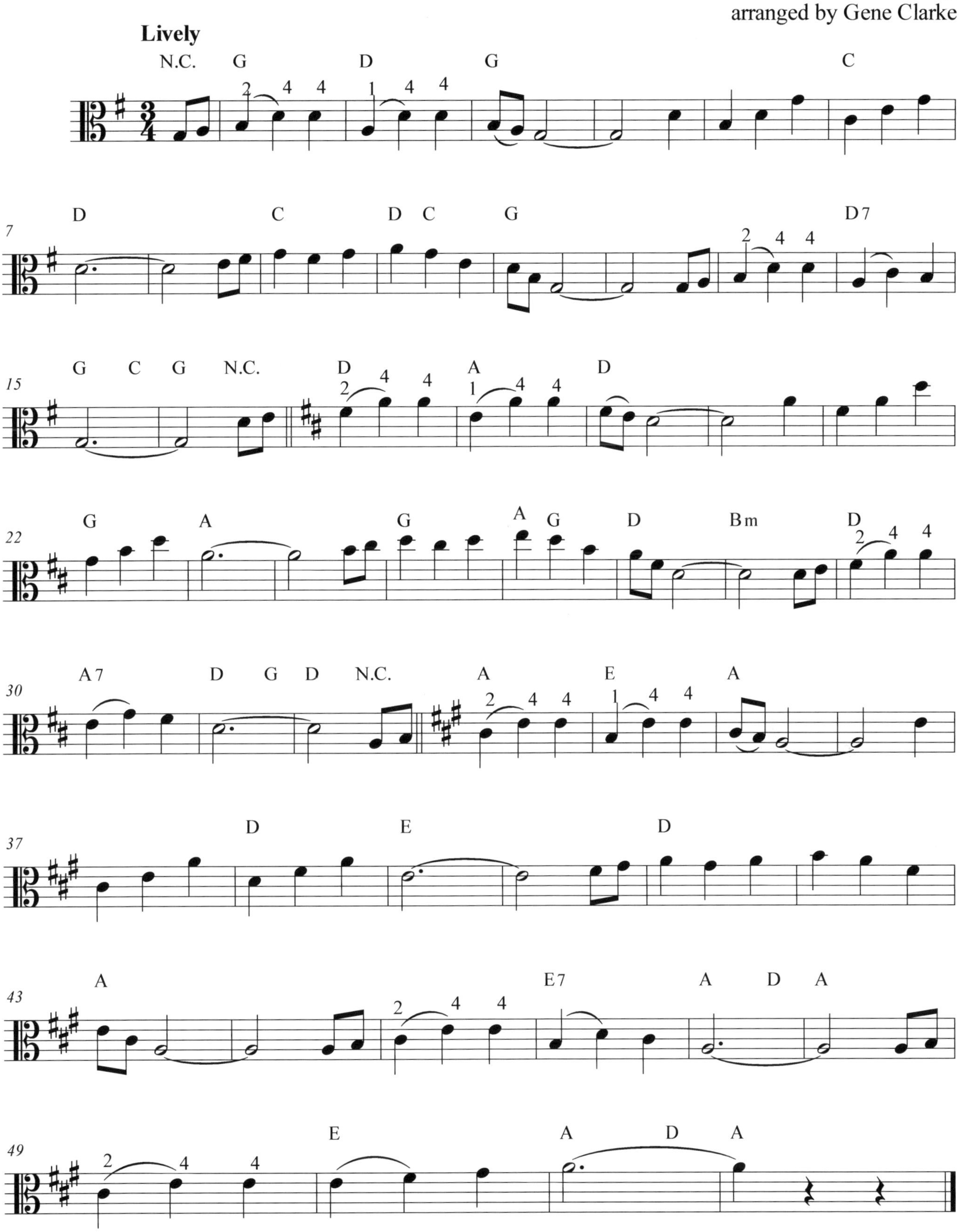

In the Days of Forty-Nine

Traditional American Ballad
arranged by Gene Clarke

Steadily-not too fast

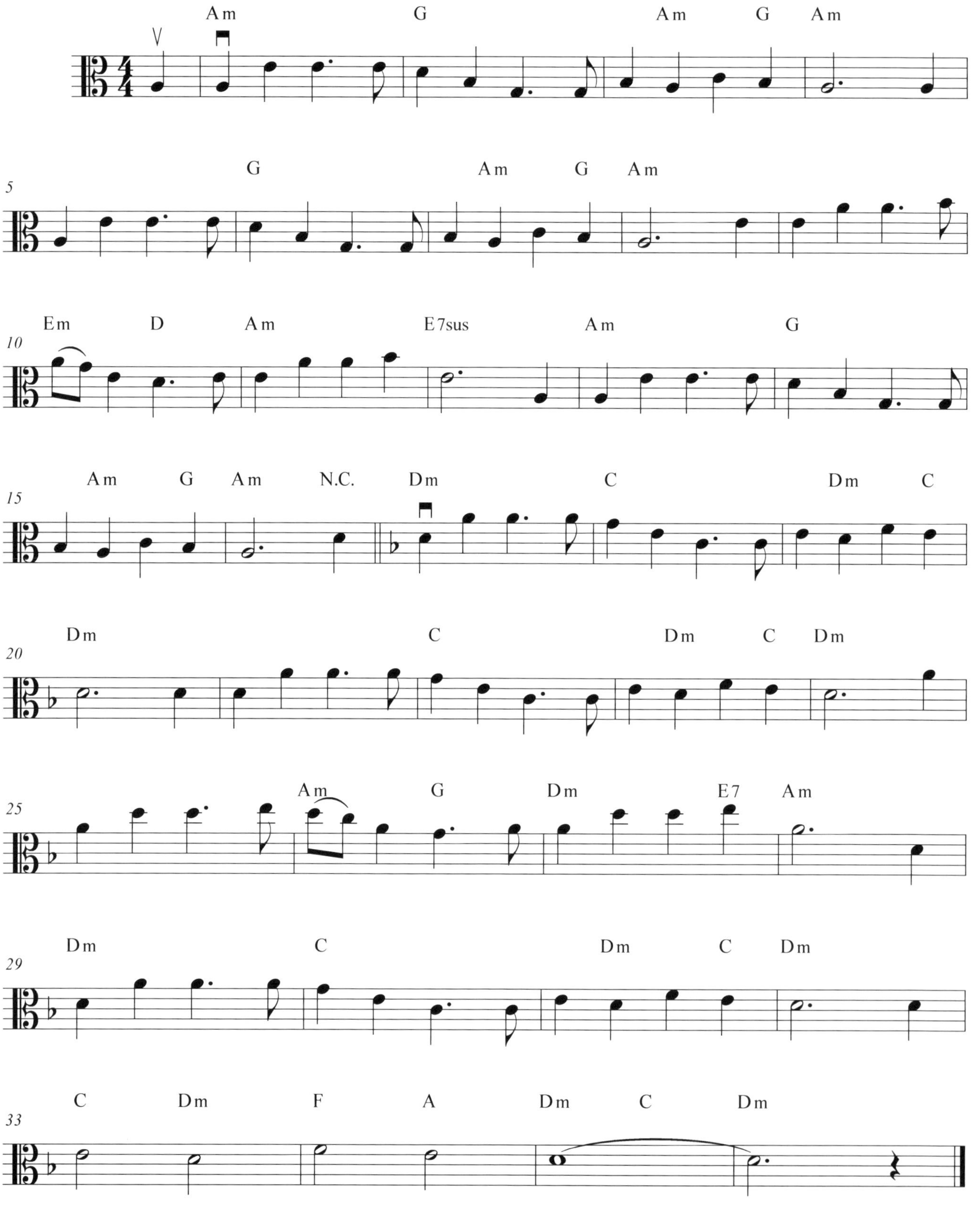

George Collins

Old English Ballad
arranged by Gene Clarke

Slowly

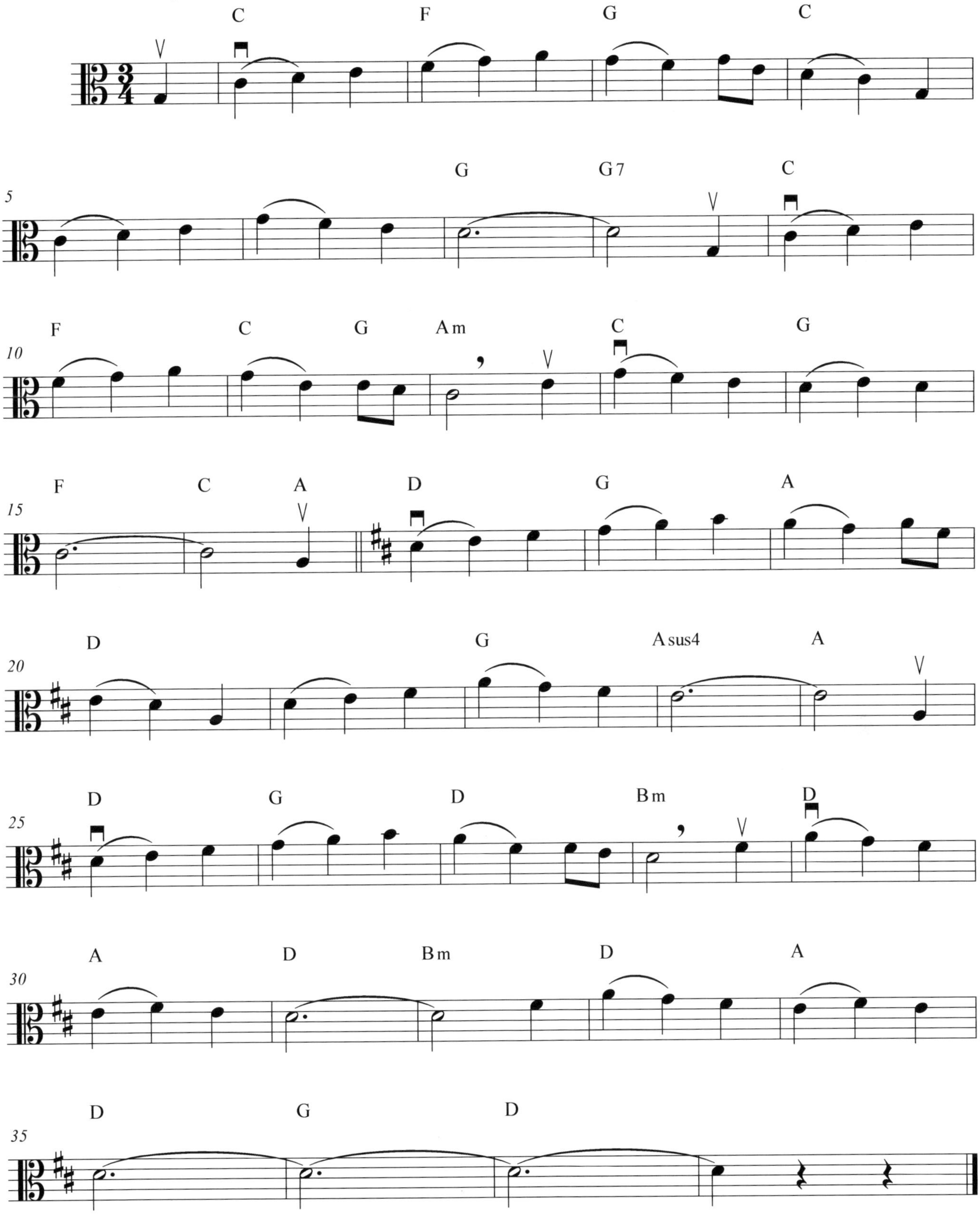

Handsome Molly

Traditional Old-Time Song
arranged by Gene Clarke

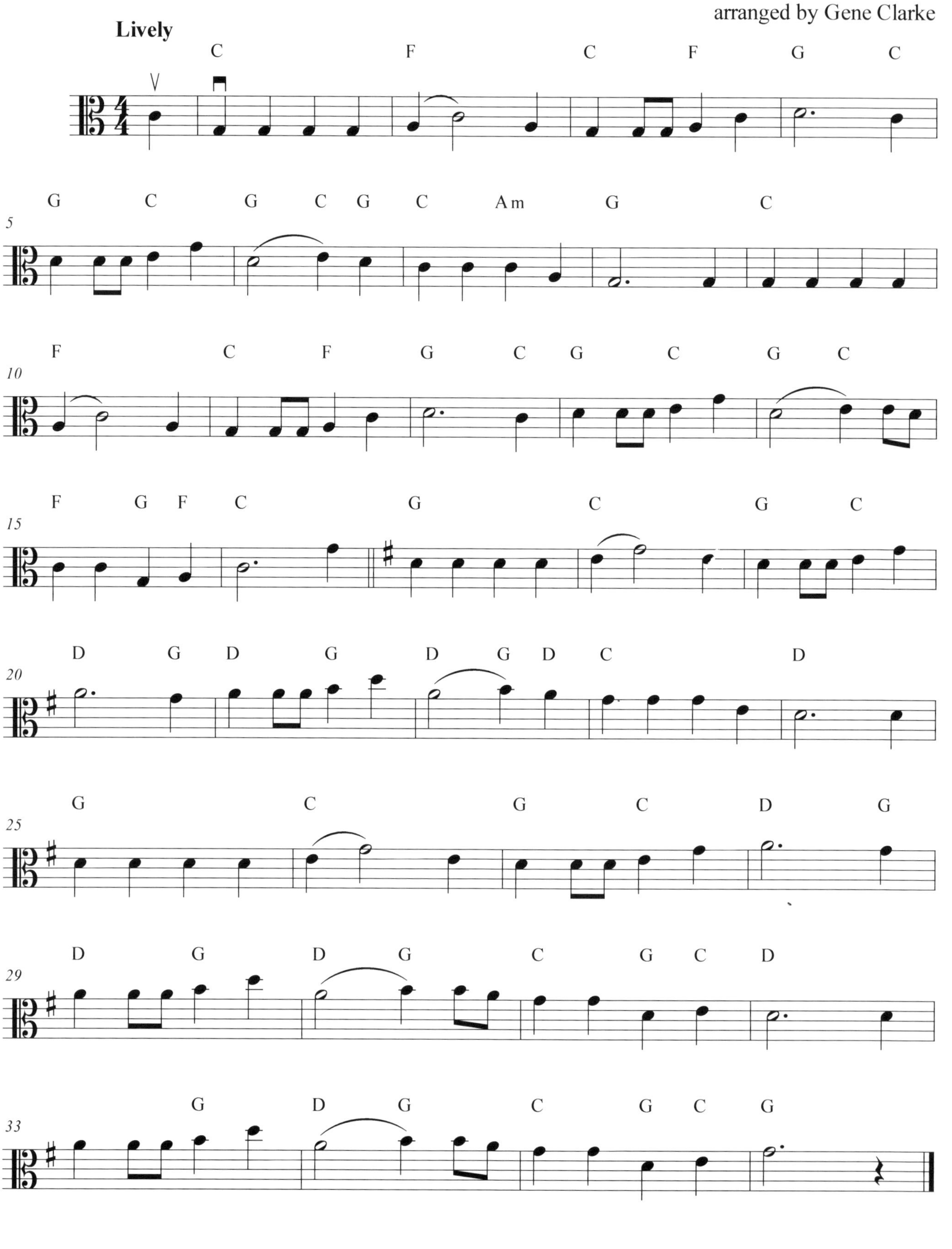

I Am a Pilgrim

Southern Gospel Tune, 1864
arranged by Gene Clarke

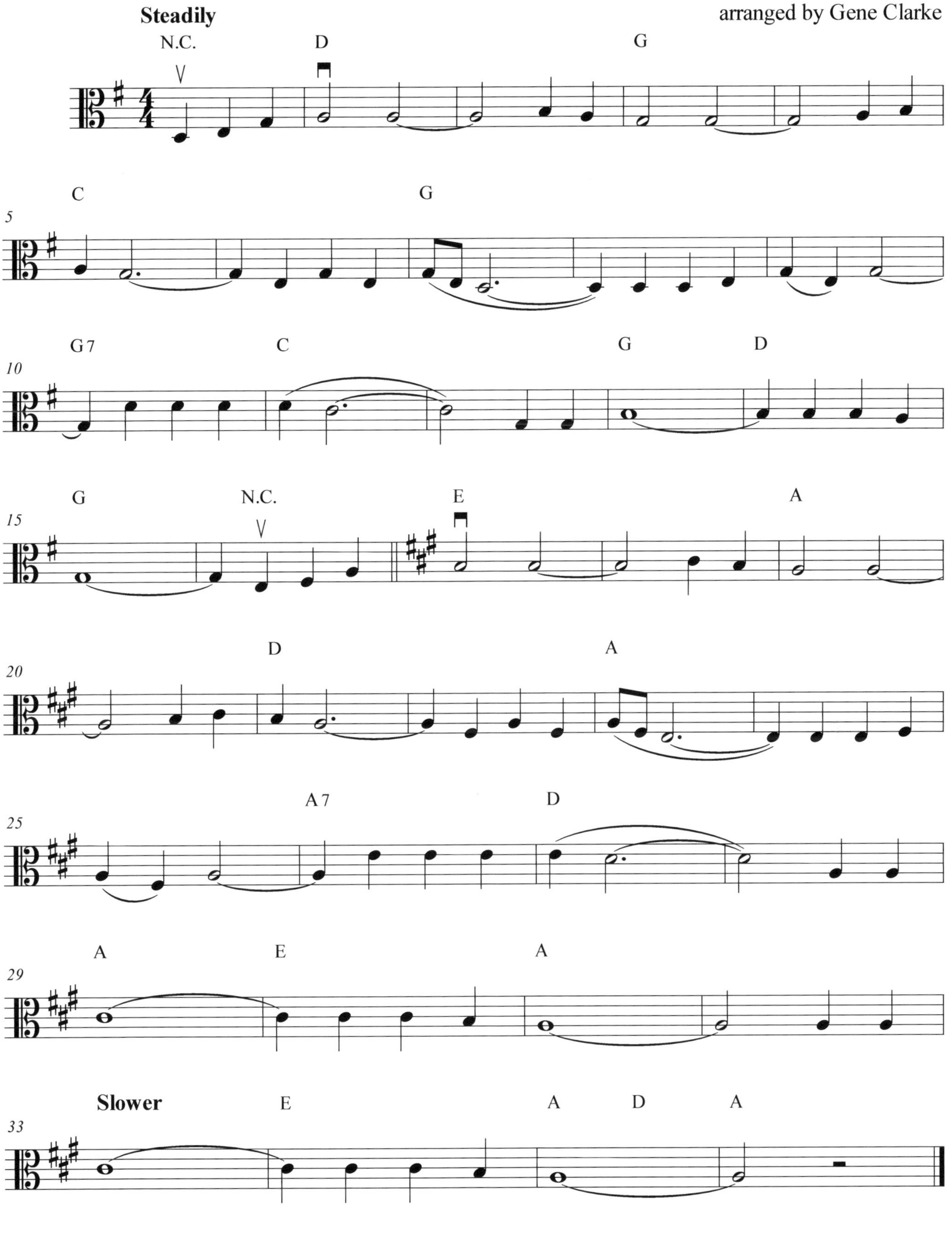

I Ride an Old Paint

Cowboy Song, Early 1900's
arranged by Gene Clarke

Loping along

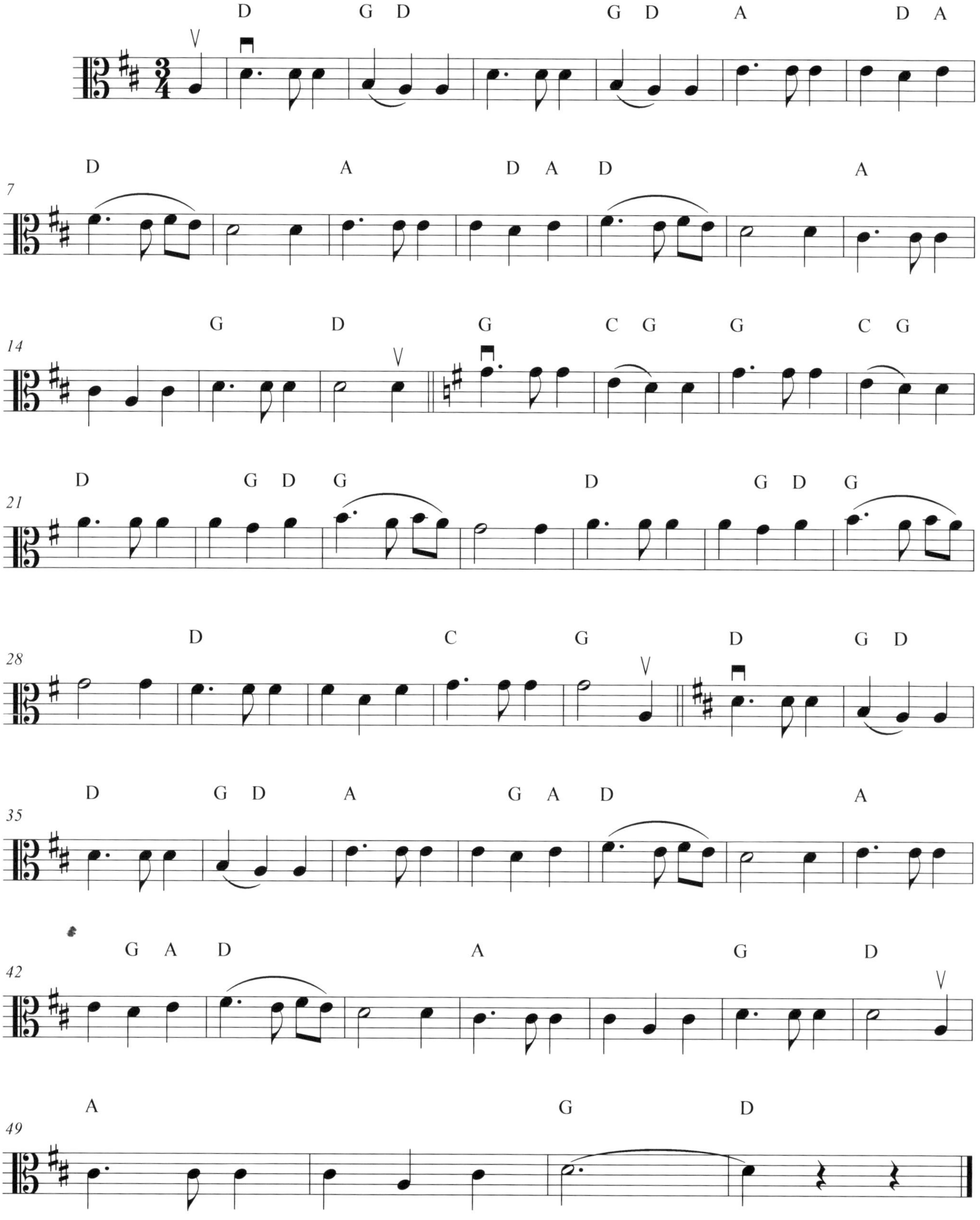

In the Good Old Summertime

Ren Shields and George Evans, 1902
arranged by Gene Clarke

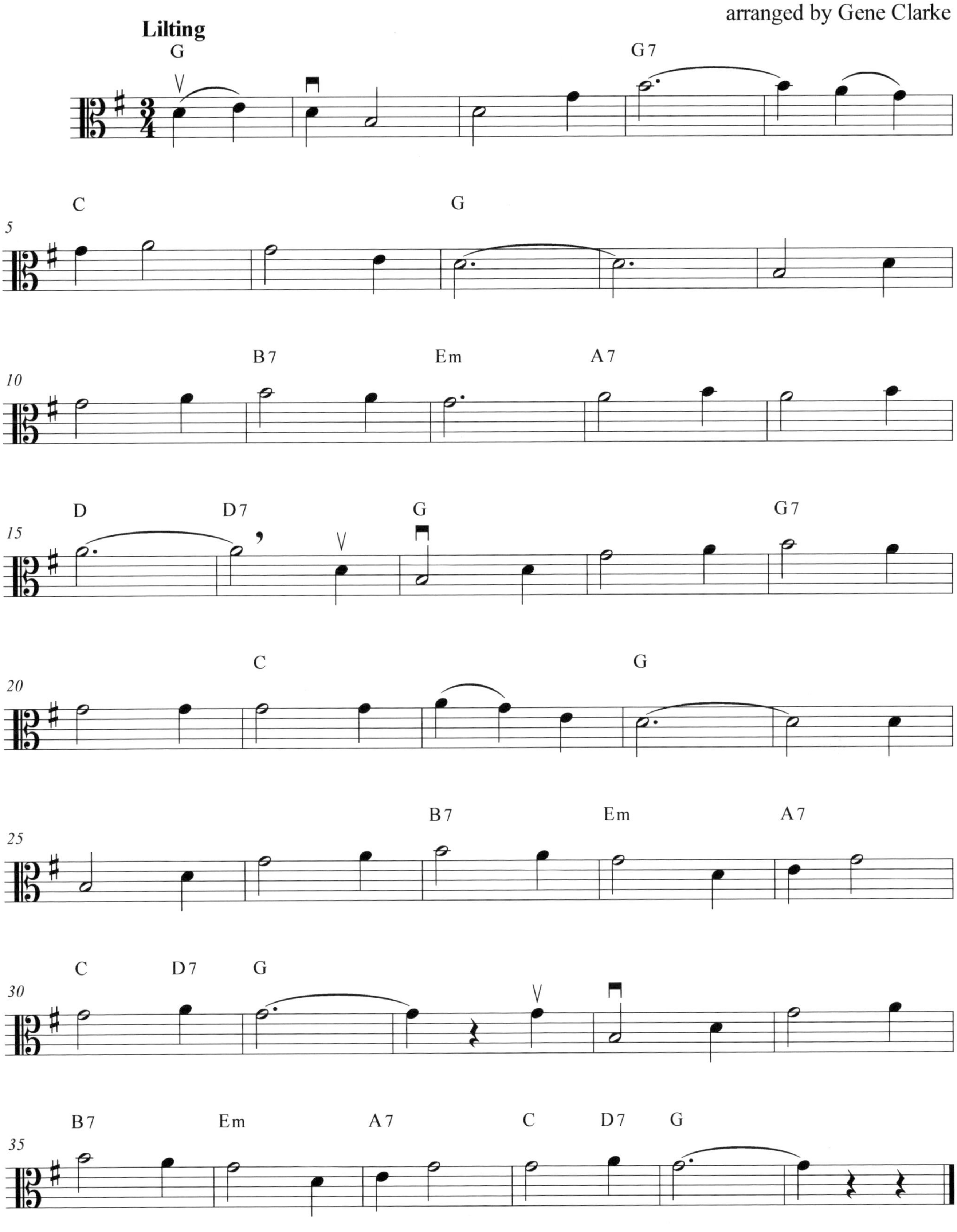

Listen to the Mockingbird

Septimus Winner, 1855
arranged by Gene Clarke

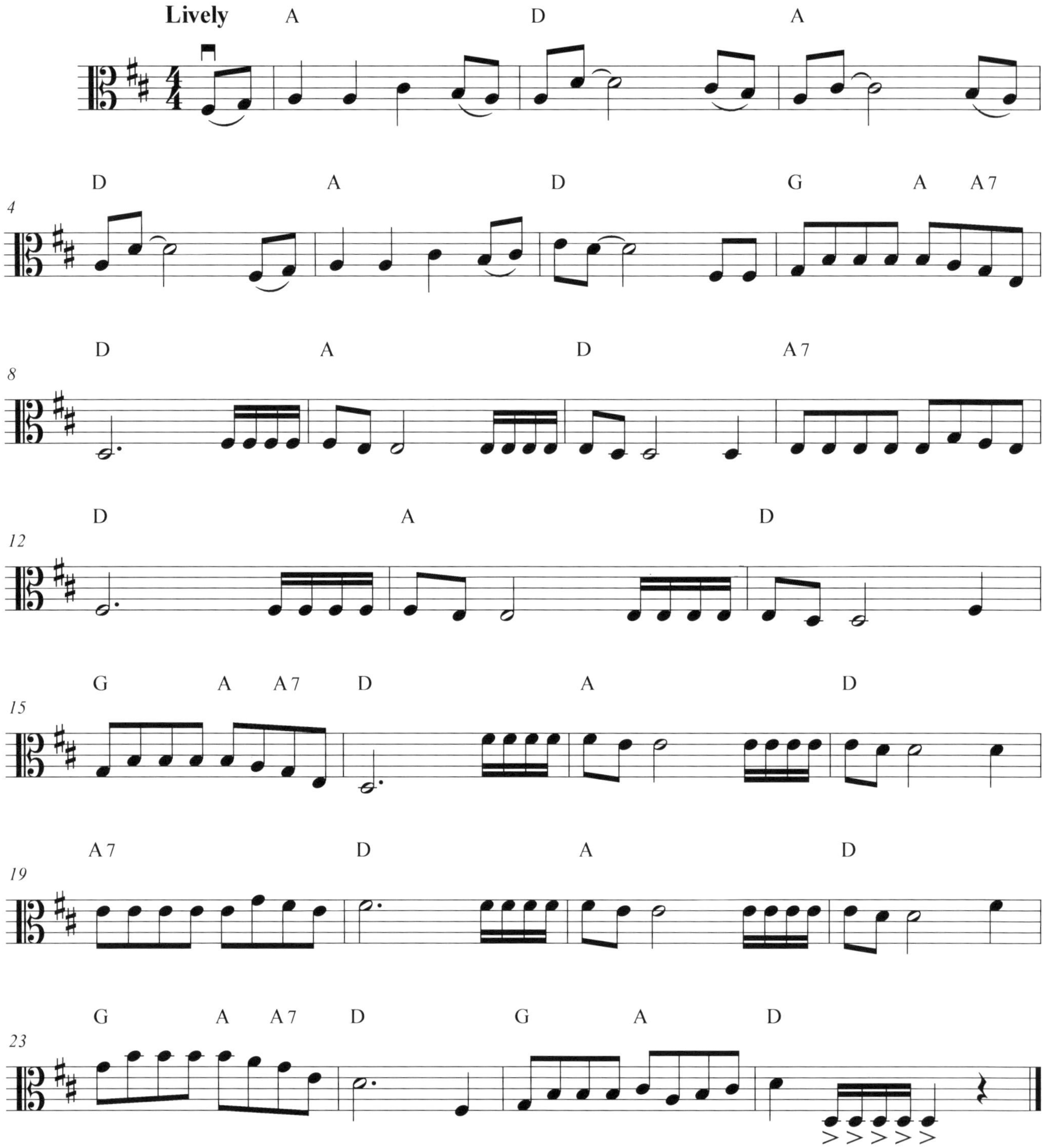

The Little Old Log Cabin in the Woods

William S. Hays, 1871
arranged by Gene Clarke

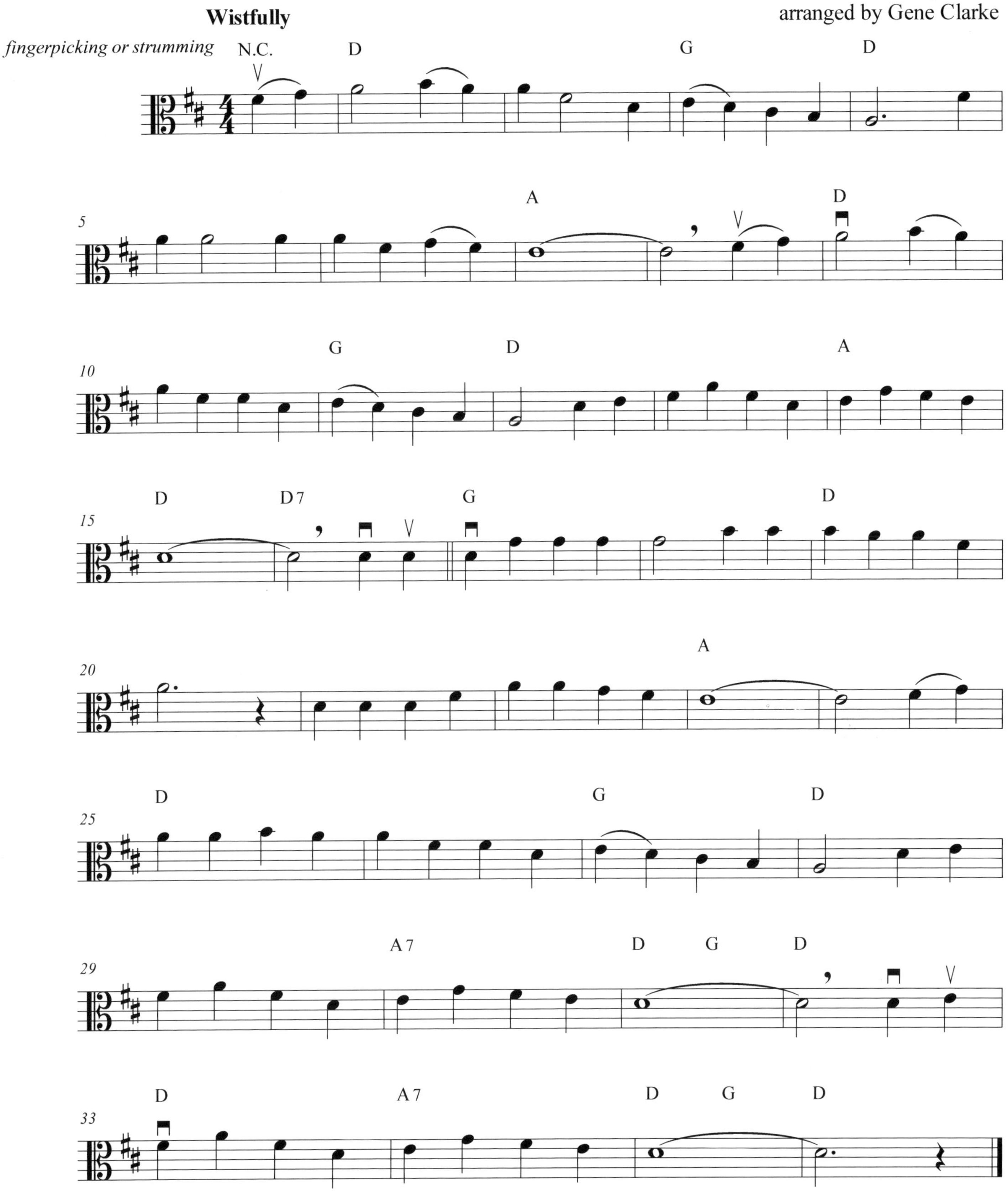

Lynchburg Town

Frank Spencer, 1848
arranged by Gene Clarke

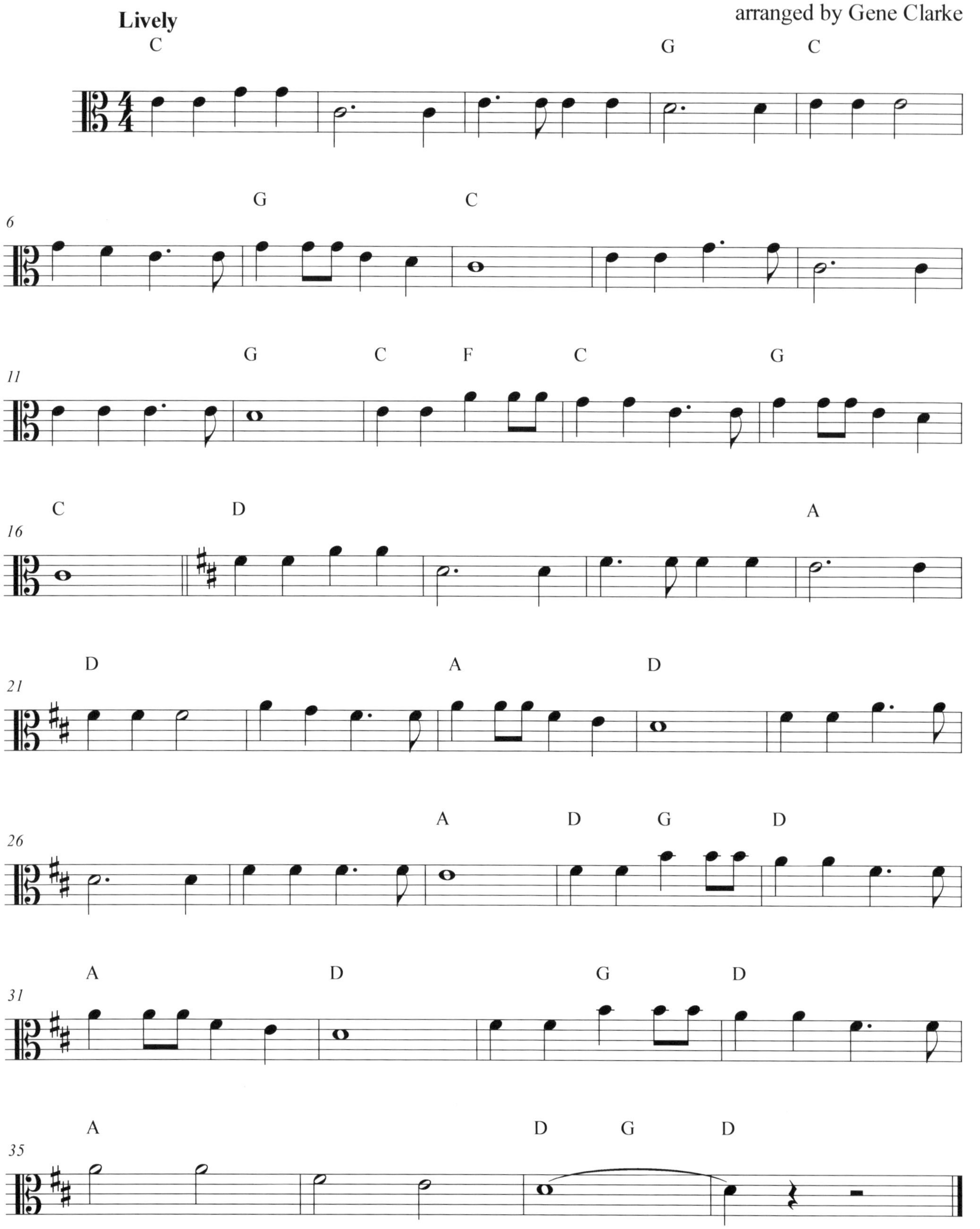

The Old Oaken Bucket

George F. Kiallmark, 1826
arranged by Gene Clarke

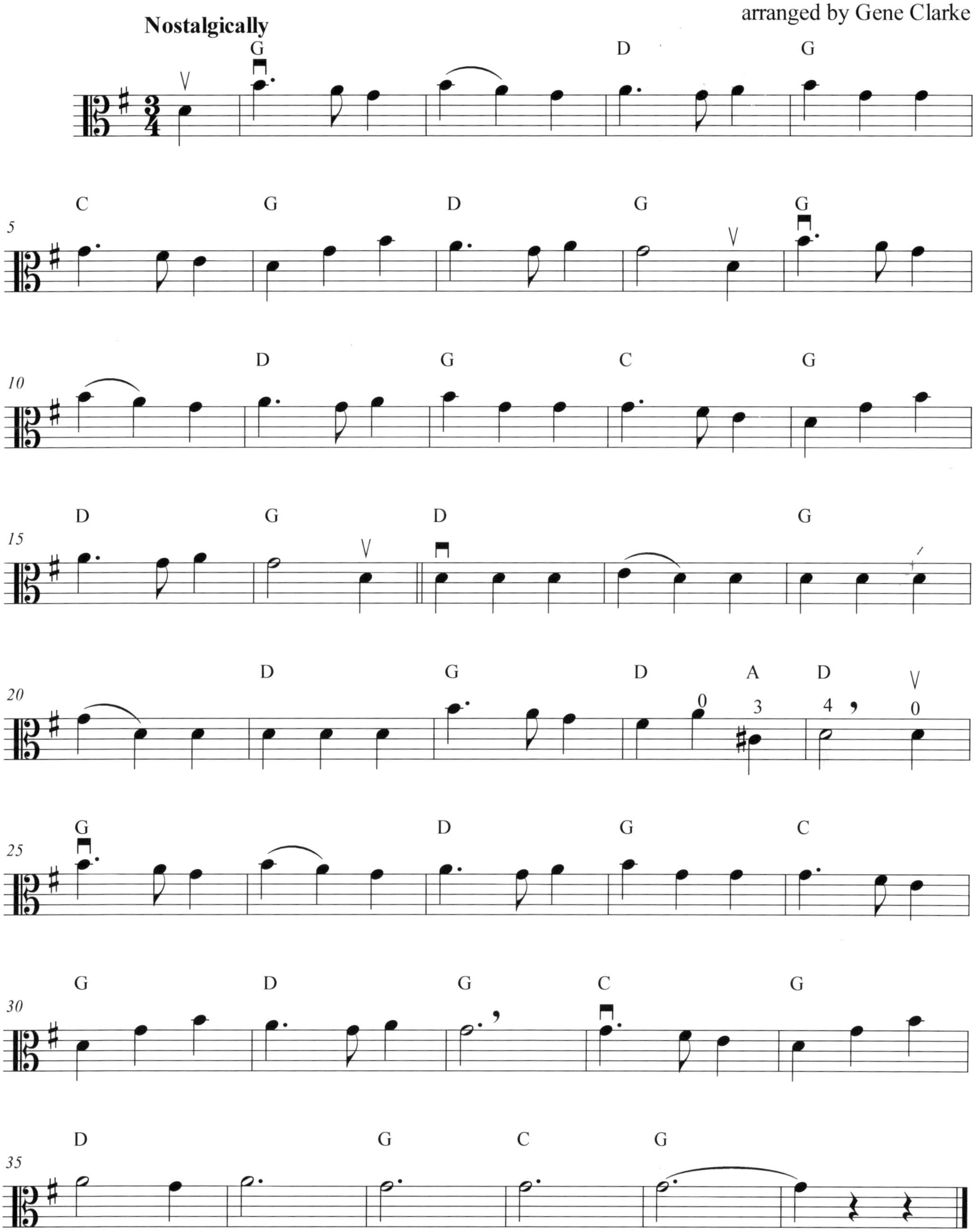

Only a Bird in a Gilded Cage

Arthur J. Lamb and Harry von Tilzer, 1900
arranged by Gene Clarke

Moderate waltz

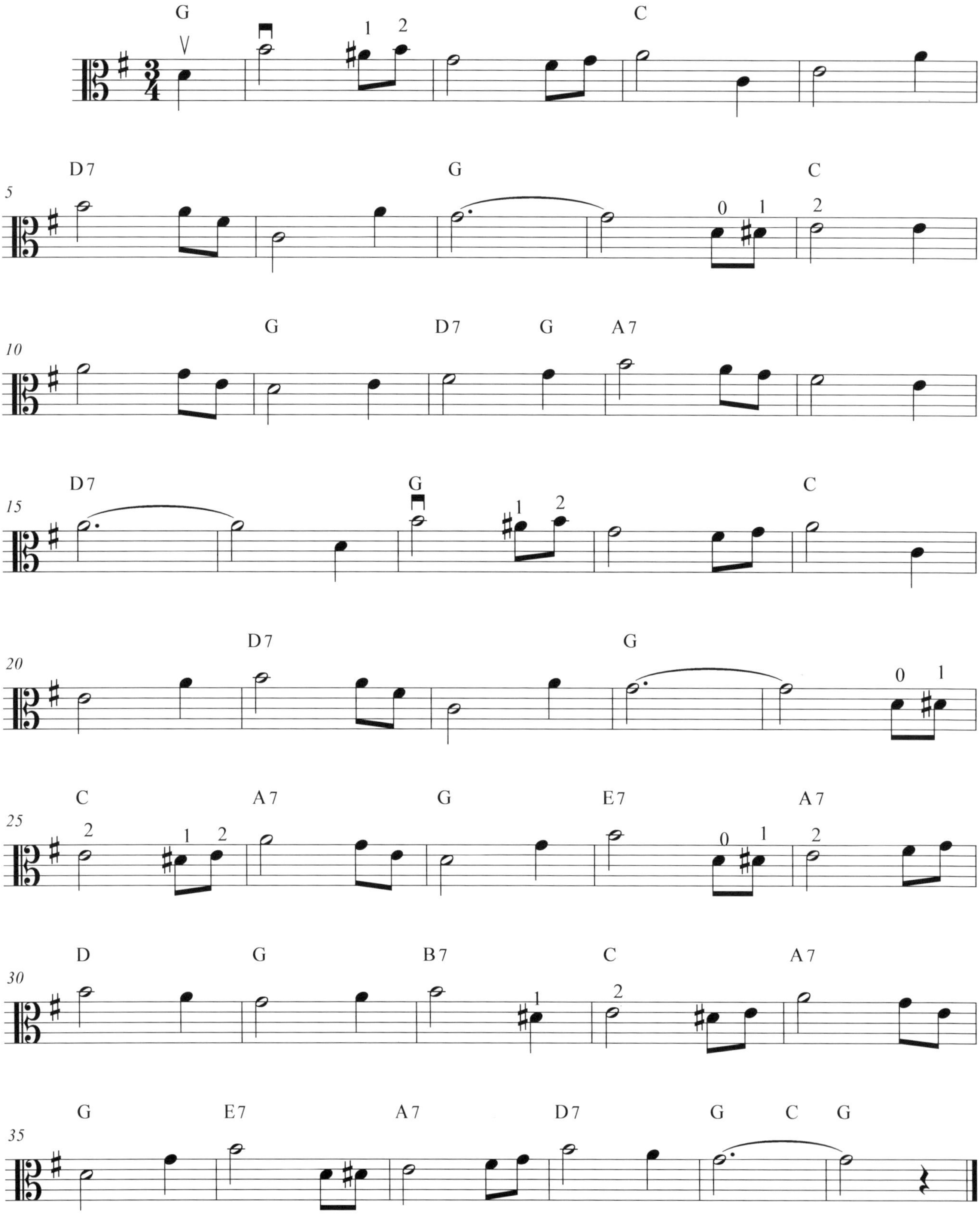

Over the Garden Wall

Harry Hunter and George D. Fox, 1879
arranged by Gene Clarke

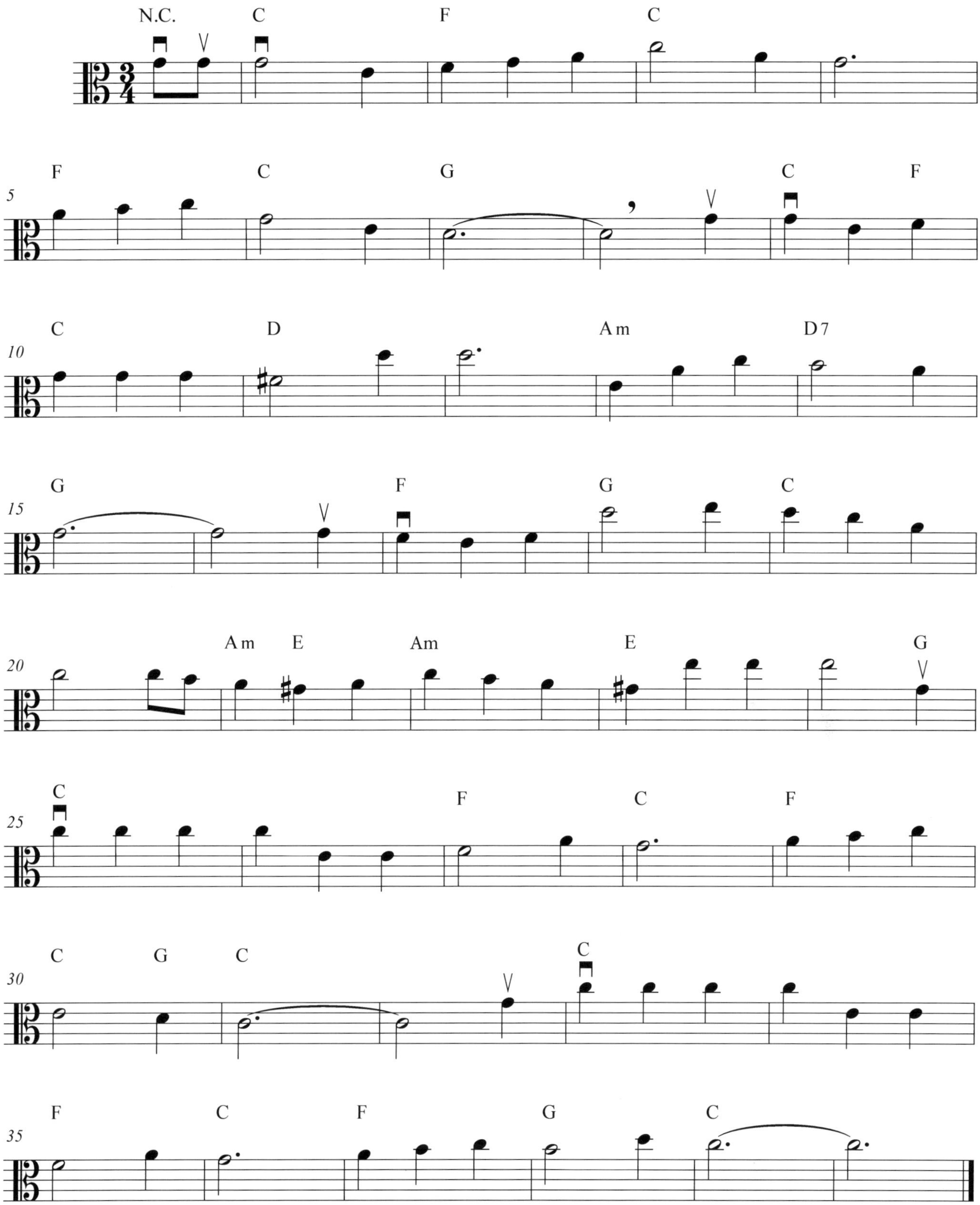

Pretty Saro

Traditional American Tune, Early 1900's
arranged by Gene Clarke

Lively

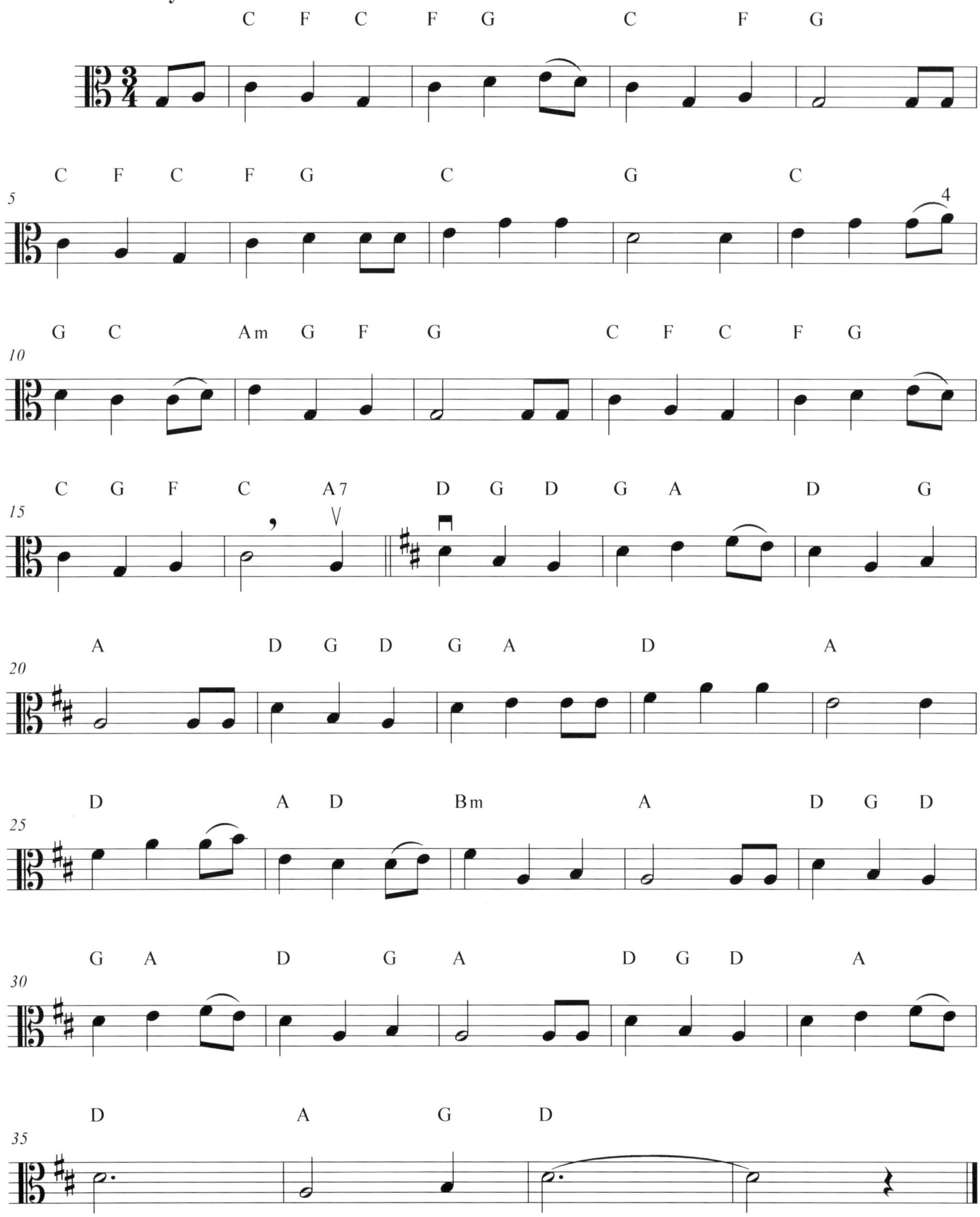

Sweet Polly Oliver

English Broadside Ballad, 1840
arranged by Gene Clarke

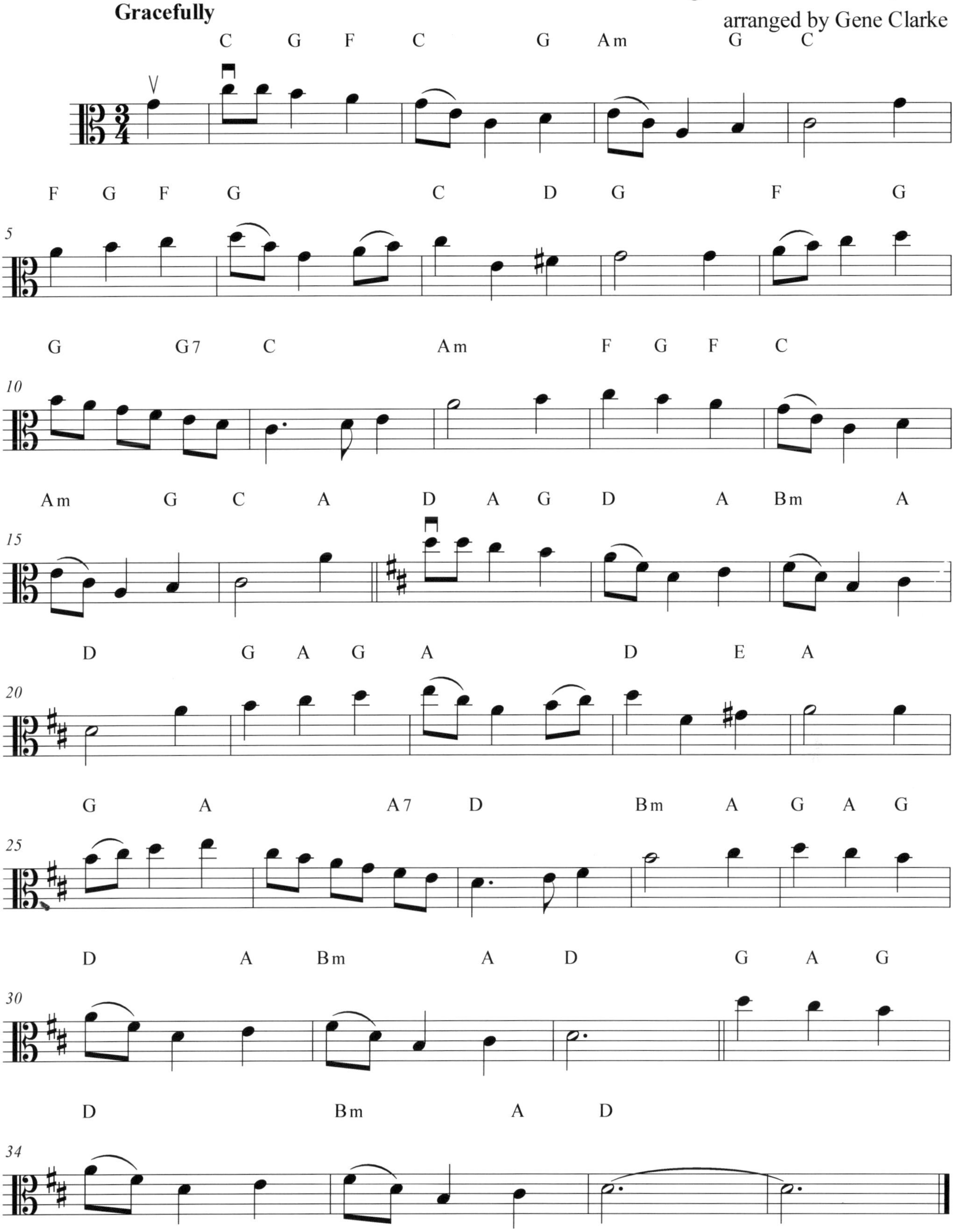

The Banks of the Ohio

19th Century Ballad

Arranged by Gene Clarke

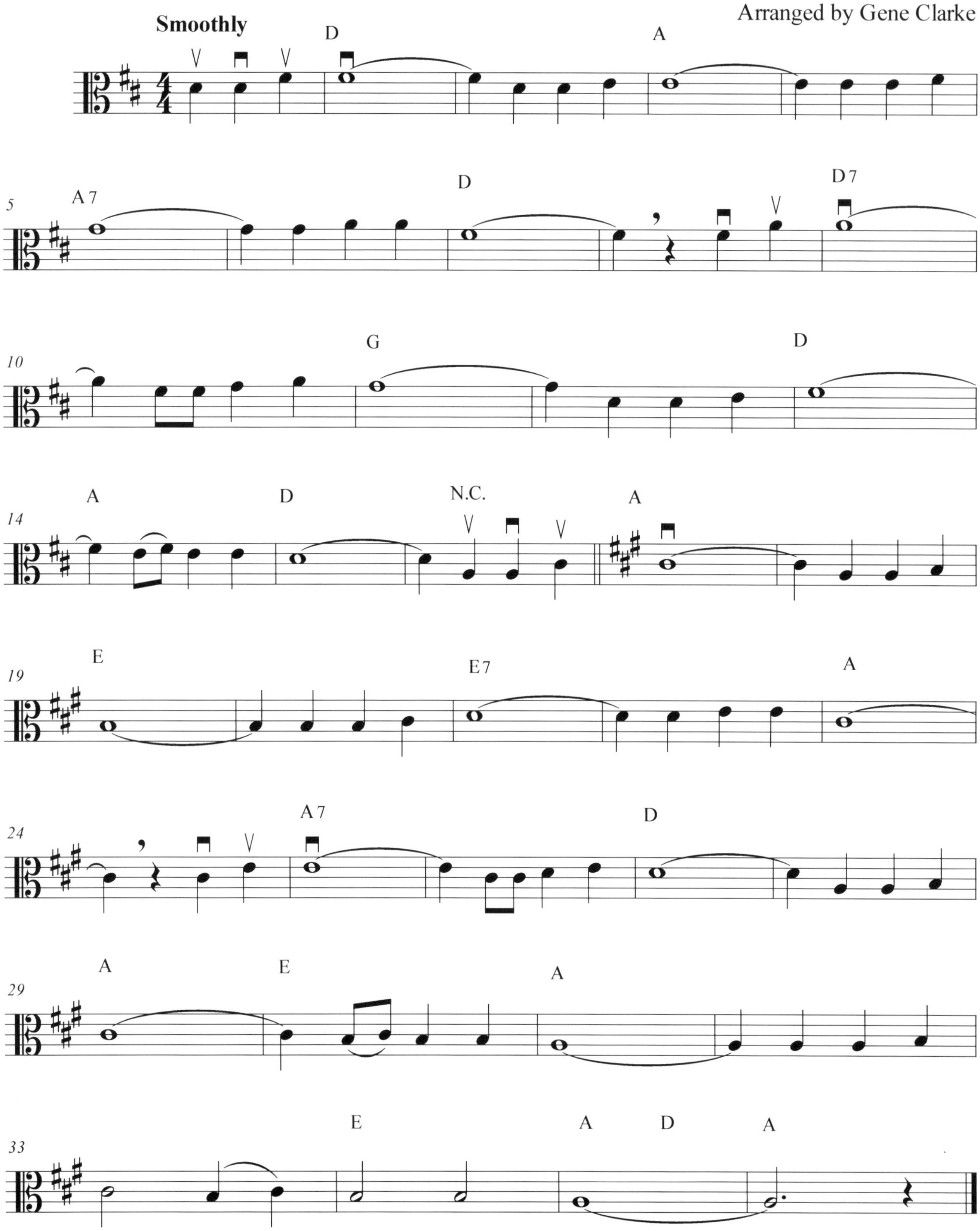

The Letter Edged in Black

Hattie Nevada, 1899
arranged by Gene Clarke

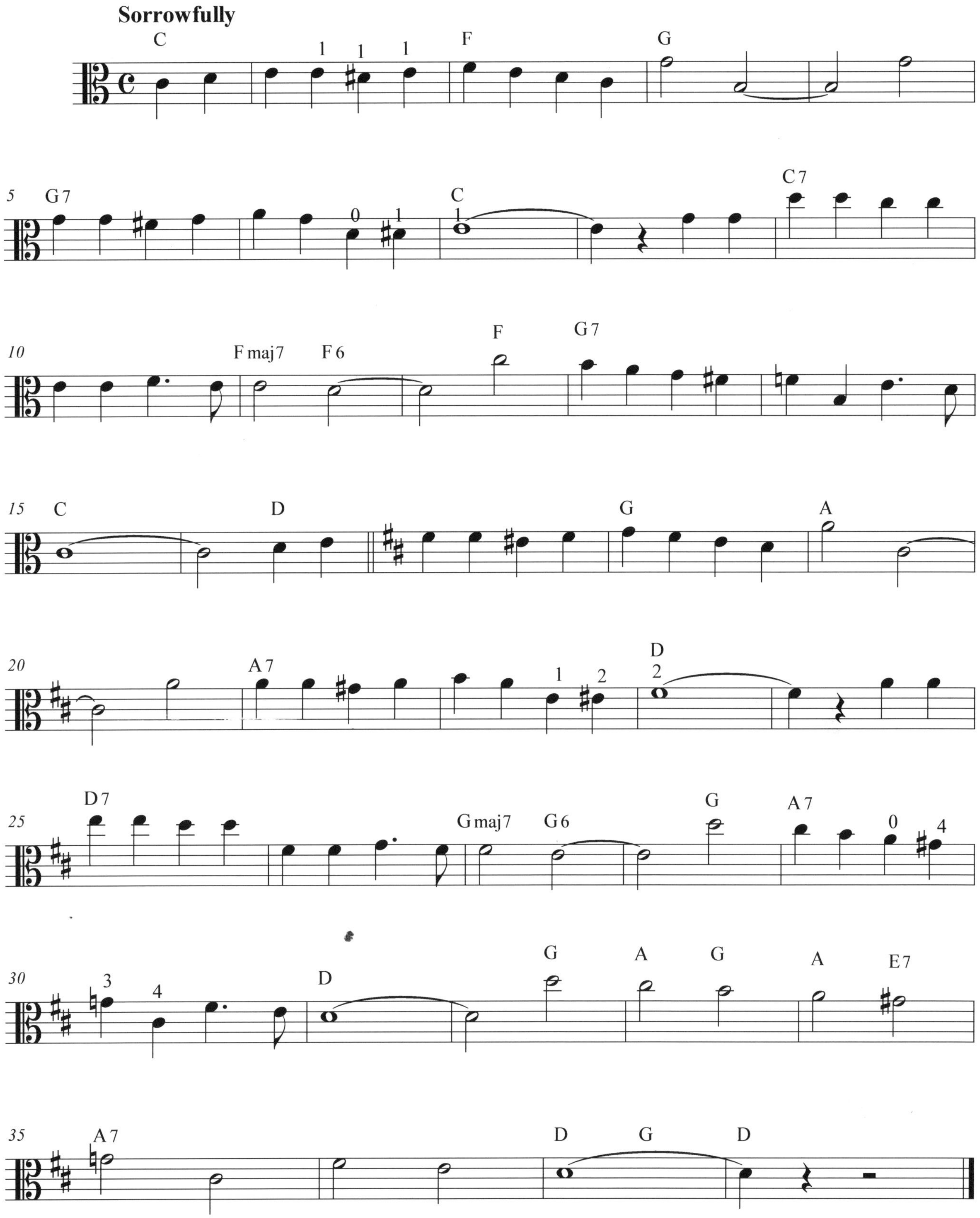

The Mermaid's Song

Scottish Air
arranged by Gene Clarke

Moderately Slow

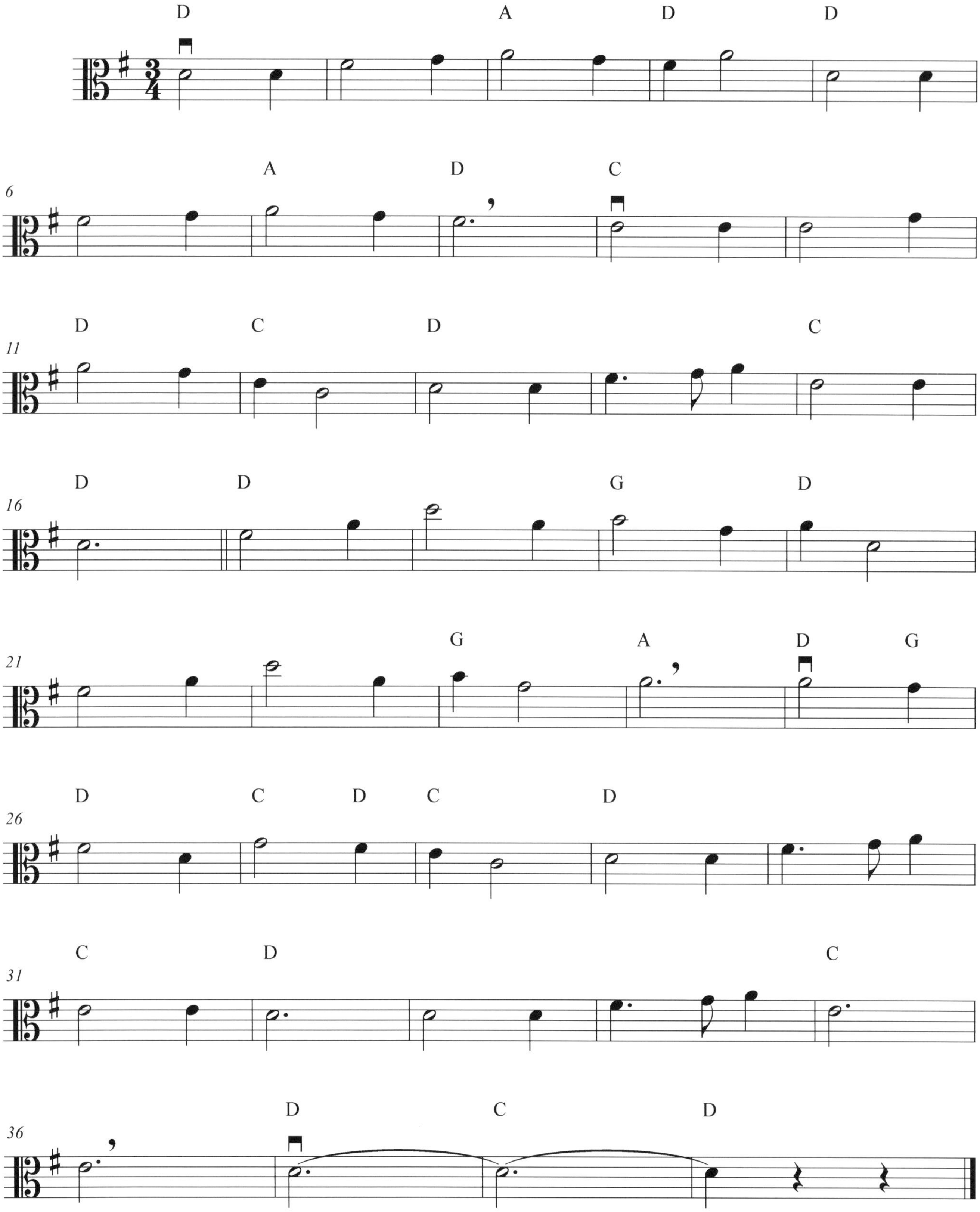

The Mist-Covered Mountains

Traditional Scottish Air
arranged by Gene Clarke

Slowly

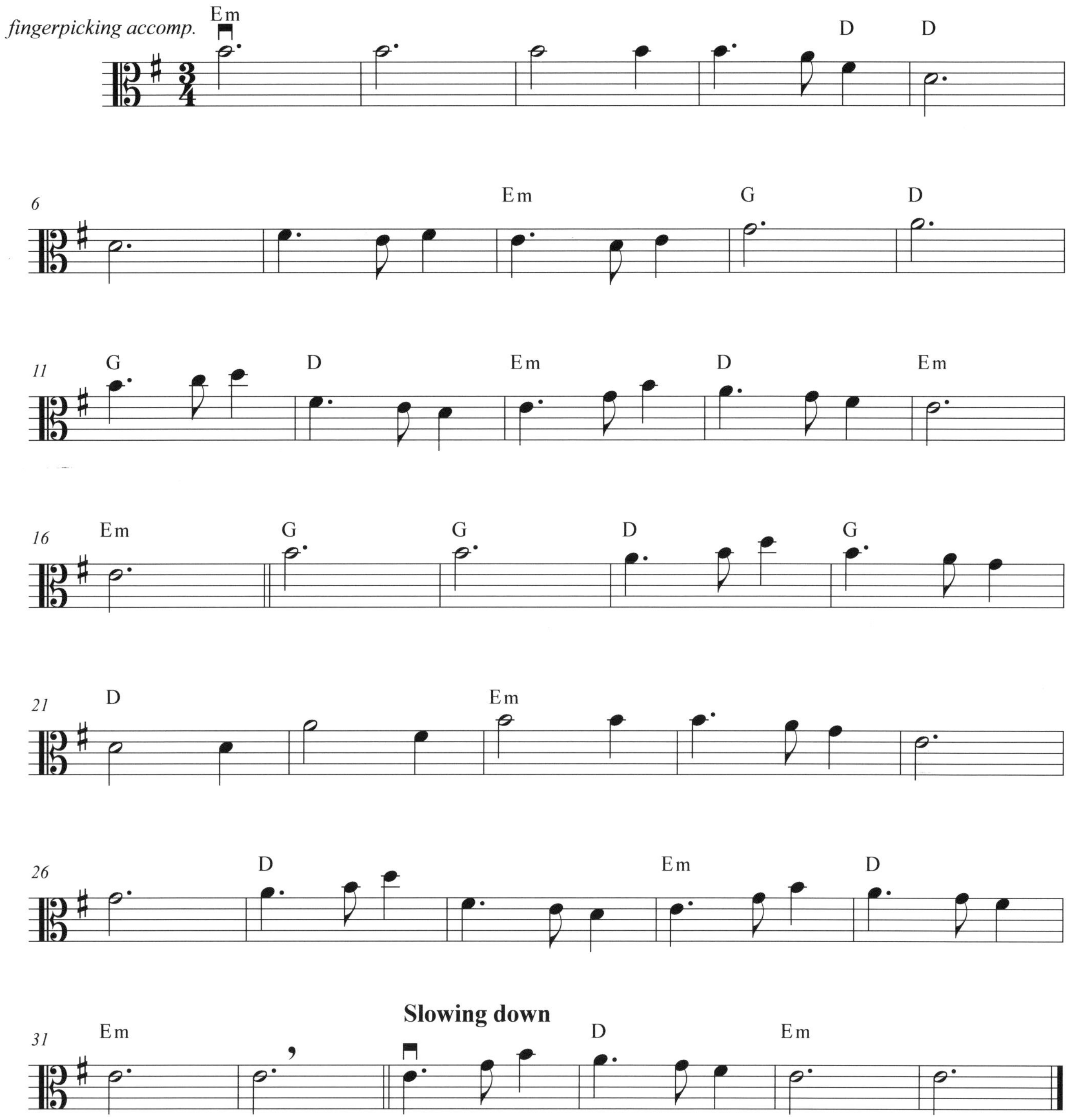

The Parting Glass

Traditional Irish Tune
arranged by Gene Clarke

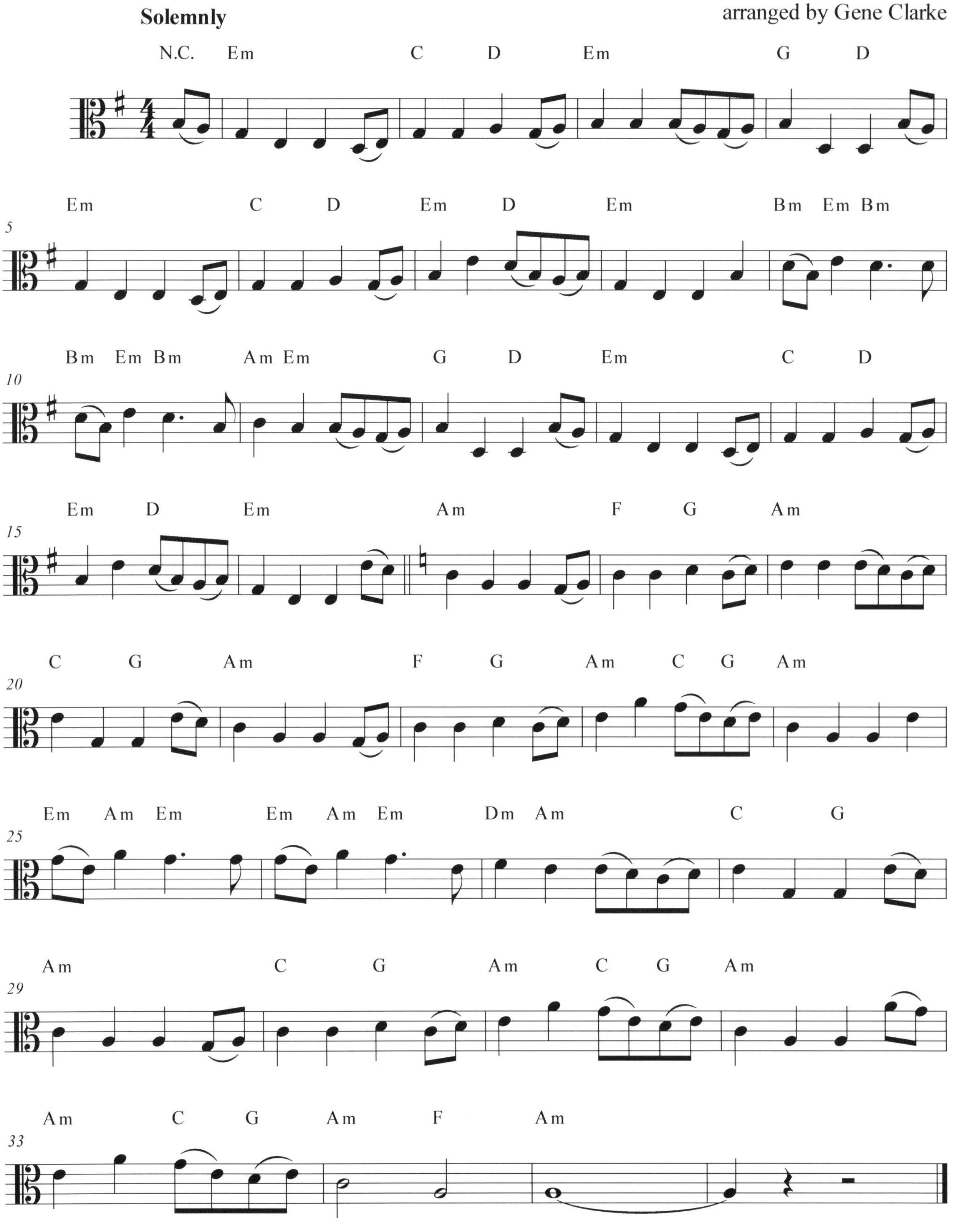

The Rose of Tralee

19th Century Irish Folk Song
arranged by Gene Clarke

Slow and sentimental

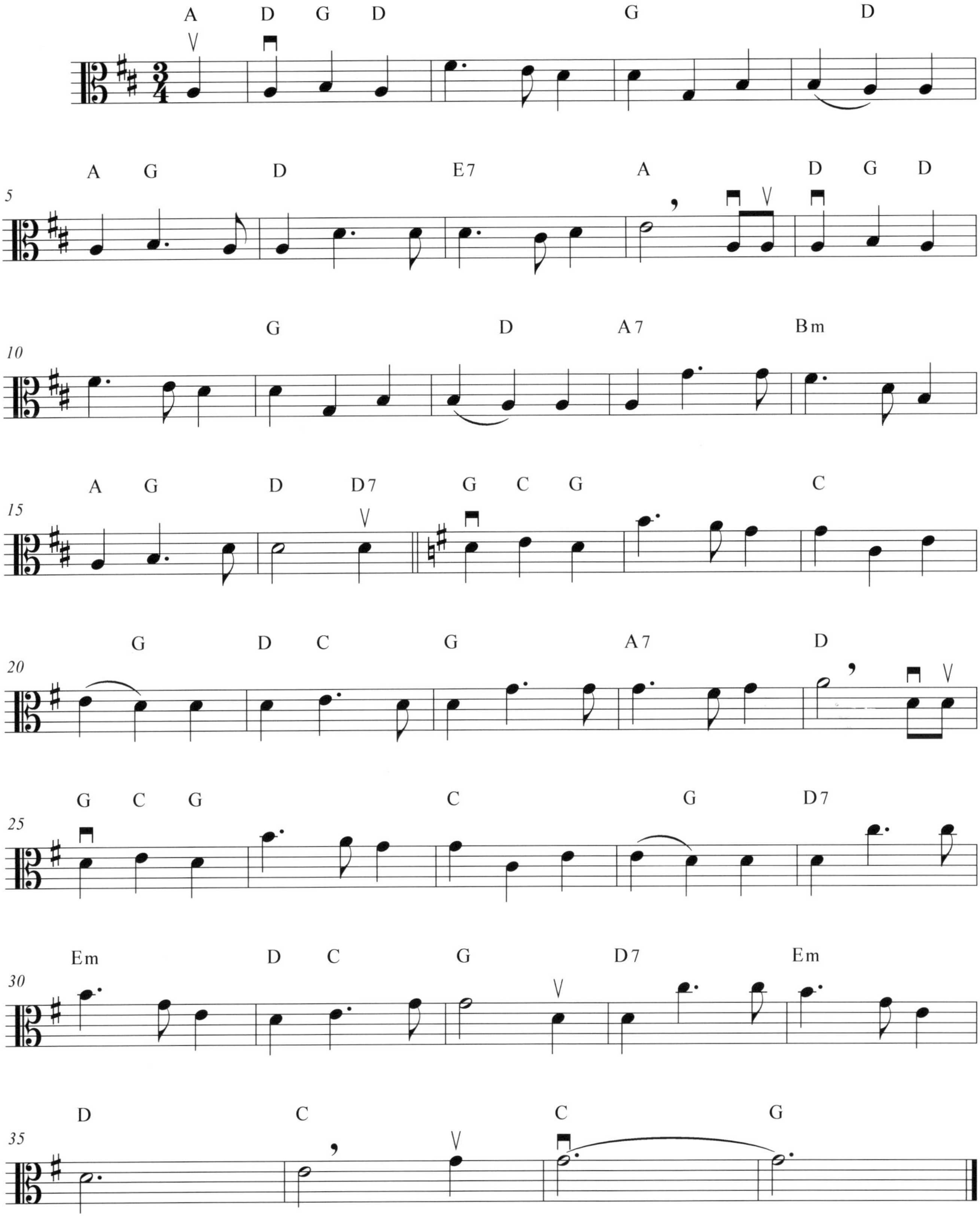

The Wagoner's Lad

Old Time Ballad, 1907
arranged by Gene Clarke

Moving along

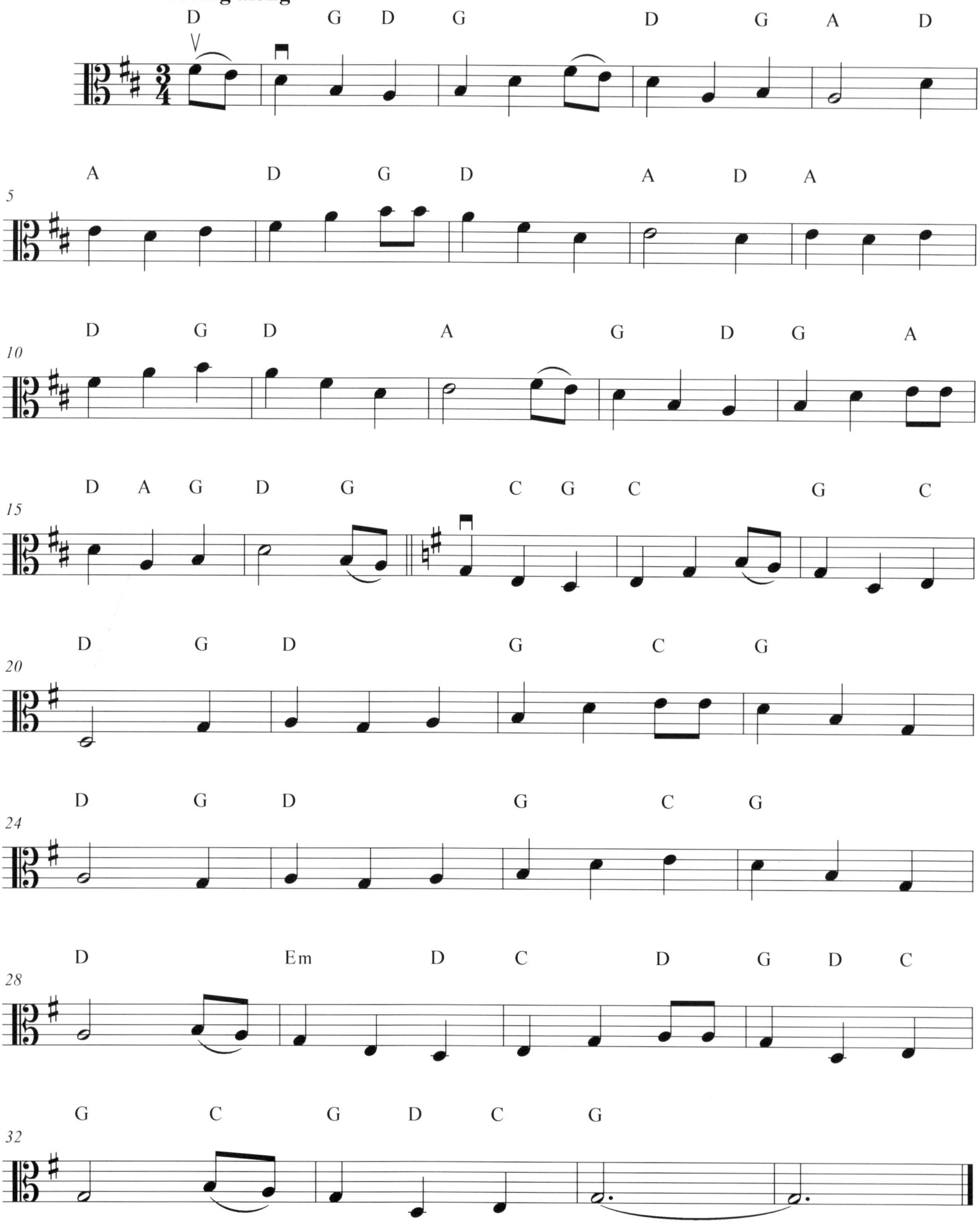